ANGEL REESE

by Maggie Hendricks

Essential Library
An Imprint of Abdo Publishing
abdobooks.com

ABDOBOOKS.COM

Published by Abdo Publishing, a division of ABDO, PO Box 398166, Minneapolis, Minnesota 55439.

Printed in China.
102025
012026

Cover Photo: Melissa Tamez/Icon Sportswire/Getty Images
Interior Photos: Andy Lyons/Getty Images Sport/Getty Images, 5, 13, 82; Kevin C. Cox/Getty Images Sport/Getty Images, 8; Ben Solomon/NCAA Photos/Getty Images, 10, 56; John Salangsang/Shutterstock Images, 15; Prince Williams/WireImage/Getty Images, 17; Amy Davis/Baltimore Sun/Getty Images, 18; Ned Dishman/NBAE/Getty Images, 21; Andrew D. Bernstein/NBAE/Getty Images, 22; Eli Pousson/Baltimore Heritage, 25; Marc Piscotty/Icon Sportswire/Getty Images, 27; Jerry Jackson/Baltimore Sun/Tribune News Service/Getty Images, 29; G. Fiume/Maryland Terrapins/Getty Images Sport/Getty Images, 31; Katherine Frey/The Washington Post/Getty Images, 34–35; Julio Cortez/AP Images, 37; Scott Wachter/NCAA Photos/Getty Images, 40; Elsa/Getty Images Sport/Getty Images, 43; Ethan Miller/Getty Images Sport/Getty Images, 47; LSU Athletics/University Images/Getty Images, 49; G. Fiume/Getty Images Sport/Getty Images, 52; Lance King/Getty Images Sport/Getty Images, 53; Eakin Howard/Getty Images Sport/Getty Images, 55; Andy Hancock/NCAA Photos/Getty Images, 61; Sarah Stier/Getty Images Sport/Getty Images, 62, 73; Brandon Todd/NBAE/Getty Images, 65; Patti McConville/Alamy, 66; Emily Johnson/NBAE/Getty Images, 69; Eileen T. Meslar/Chicago Tribune/Tribune News Service/Getty Images, 74; David Sherman/NBAE/Getty Images, 77, 91; David Warren/Sipa USA/Alamy Live News/Alamy, 79; Juan Ocampo/NBAE/Getty Images, 87; Patrick McDermott/Getty Images Sport/Getty Images, 88; Anatoliy Tesouro/Shutterstock Images, 93; Javier Vicencio/Eyepix Group/Alamy, 94; Megan Briggs/Getty Images Sport/Getty Images, 97; Joe Buglewicz/Getty Images Sport/Getty Images, 98

Editor: Riley Madsen
Series Designer: Karli Hughes

Library of Congress Control Number: 2025939221

PUBLISHER'S CATALOGING-IN-PUBLICATION DATA

Names: Hendricks, Maggie, author.
Title: Angel Reese / by Maggie Hendricks
Description: Minneapolis, Minnesota: Abdo Publishing, 2026 | Series: Modern stars | Includes online resources and index.
Identifiers: ISBN 9781098298074 (lib. bdg.) | ISBN 9798384931874 (ebook)
Subjects: LCSH: Reese, Angel, 2002- --Juvenile literature. | Women basketball players--United States--Biography--Juvenile literature. | African American women basketball players--Biography--Juvenile literature. | Female athletes--Biography--Juvenile literature. | Chicago Sky (Basketball team)--Juvenile literature.
Classification: DDC 796.323--dc23

CONTENTS

CHAPTER ONE

THE FINAL FOUR

With just a few seconds left in the game, Angel Reese waved her hand in front of her face, pointed to her ring finger, and then ran toward the sideline to hug her coach, Kim Mulkey. These two women had just accomplished what had seemed unlikely when Reese transferred to Louisiana State University (LSU). The Tigers had just won the 2023 National Collegiate Athletic Association (NCAA) championship in women's basketball, the school's first. Confetti rained down from the ceiling of the American Airlines Center in Dallas, Texas, to celebrate the win. Reese continued to find teammates to hug.

Reese attended a postgame press conference after LSU's win. She wore a T-shirt declaring LSU the national champion. She also brought a rhinestone crown and set it on the table in front of her.

With each win in the women's March Madness tournament, Reese and the Tigers came one step closer to the championship. >>

NCAA
SEC
LSU
10

The accessory suggested that she was queen of the game, a title she had earned with her March Madness performance. This tournament determines the yearly NCAA championship. She was named the tournament's Most Outstanding Player, and she had secured not just the win but the interest of millions of Americans. The game broke records for women's basketball television ratings.

PATH TO THE CHAMPIONSHIP

LSU's journey to the title started a year earlier, when Reese decided to transfer from the University of Maryland to LSU. Playing for Mulkey, the Tigers put up an exceptional regular-season record of 27–1. Their sole loss was to the University of South Carolina. Next came the Southeastern Conference (SEC) tournament. The SEC is one of the toughest conferences in women's college basketball. South Carolina, the 2022 NCAA champion, belongs to the SEC, as does longtime powerhouse the University of Tennessee. Playing in Greenville, South Carolina, LSU lost in the semifinals of the SEC tournament to Tennessee 69–67.

"I have a voice, and I'm not going to stop using my voice for the people that know that I am making an impact."[1]

—Angel Reese, August 2023

But the NCAA Tournament, the biggest competition in women's college basketball, still lay ahead. With its loss in the SEC semifinals, LSU was given a number three seed, or ranking, in the NCAA Tournament. The University of Indiana and the University of Utah were seeded above the Tigers in their section of the bracket.

SOUTHEASTERN CONFERENCE

While at LSU, Reese competed in the SEC. In the NCAA, teams can be a part of conferences, which set up scheduling, championships, and television deals. The SEC is one of the strongest conferences in college sports. SEC teams routinely win national championships in an array of sports, including football, men's basketball, women's basketball, and gymnastics. The conference was founded in 1932 and has expanded three times. It even has its own television network.

LSU would be playing on its home court for the first two rounds of the tournament. The team easily beat the University of Hawaii 73–50 in the first round. Reese scored 34 points and had three blocks and three steals in the win. Two days later, Reese was again a star in LSU's second-round win over the University of Michigan. Playing in front of a huge crowd at the Pete Maravich Center in Baton Rouge, Louisiana, she scored 25 points and grabbed 24 rebounds.

With this win, Reese and the Tigers moved into the Sweet 16 round of the tournament. They headed back to Greenville, where they had lost just weeks before to the

During most of her basketball career, including at LSU, Reese played the forward position.

University of Tennessee. This time, LSU faced off against the Utah Utes. Reese recorded double digits in two statistical categories, a feat known as a double-double, with 17 points and 12 rebounds. LSU went on a run midway through the fourth quarter, securing the lead. The Tigers beat the Utes 66–63 to earn a spot in the Elite Eight.

On the other side of the bracket, Indiana lost in the second round to the University of Miami Hurricanes. Miami went on to beat Villanova University. This set up a showdown between Miami and LSU. The winner would head to the Final Four.

LSU dominated a defensive matchup. Neither team shot the ball very well. LSU's Kateri Poole made the only three-pointer all game for either team, despite the Tigers and Hurricanes totaling 27 three-point attempts. Still, LSU found a way to get the 54–42 win. Reese had 13 points and 18 rebounds. After the game, Reese, her teammates, and Mulkey followed the NCAA basketball tradition of cutting down the net after winning a spot in the Final Four.

With this win, Reese and LSU headed to Dallas for their next game. Three other teams had also earned their trips to Dallas. These were the South Carolina Gamecocks, LSU's rival in the SEC; the University of Iowa Hawkeyes, a team led by star player Caitlin Clark; and the Virginia Tech Hokies, a team whose shooting skills could take over a game at any minute.

NCAA TOURNAMENT

Also known as Women's March Madness, the NCAA women's basketball tournament is held every spring to decide which team is the best in all of Division I women's basketball. Teams qualify either by winning their conference tournaments or by being selected by the NCAA Women's Basketball Committee. Sixty-eight teams from across the country made the tournament in 2023. The teams are slotted into a bracket, with the teams viewed as the strongest getting the top seeds. The tournament is single elimination, meaning that when a team loses, it is out.

Angel Reese won the tip-off to start LSU's game against Virginia Tech.

The Final Four is more than just the basketball games. Fans, coaches, media, and other people working in the sport all flock to the Final Four. So do Women's National Basketball Association (WNBA) general managers, who are scouting for future professional players.

While the games are the focus of the week, there are also parties and events sponsored by brands that support women's basketball, such as Nike and Gatorade. All the big names in women's basketball were there. The spotlight was on Reese, Mulkey, and LSU.

LSU's Final Four game pitted the Tigers against Virginia Tech. The Tigers struggled early, and the Hokies led after three quarters. But a run early in the fourth quarter—helped by six points from Reese—gave the

Tigers the lead. Reese said after the game, "Coach told us in the huddle, 'Play these next two minutes, and see how far it can take you.' Those next two minutes, we went on a 7–0 run. It was listening to those coaches and trusting them. [Mulkey] has been here before. We have to trust them."[2]

LSU's defense held Georgia Amoore, Virginia Tech's sharpshooter, to just 17 points. Reese finished with 24 points, 12 rebounds, and three steals. With the 79–72 victory, LSU was one win away from the school's first-ever championship in women's basketball. "It's like a dream. It still hasn't hit me that I'm at the Final Four," Reese said. "I'm just not even believing this right now. It's crazy how much my life has changed in one year."[3]

Right after LSU's win over Virginia Tech, Iowa pulled an upset over top-seeded South Carolina. The Gamecocks, whose lineup featured future WNBA number one draft pick Aliyah Boston, hadn't lost a game that season. But in the Final Four, South Carolina struggled to make shots. Boston found herself in foul trouble, scoring only eight points.

Meanwhile, Clark scored 41 points for Iowa as the Hawkeyes took out the Gamecocks. Clark, who had won several Player of the Year awards just before the Final

Four started, pointed out how big the game was, not only for Iowa but also for the sport. "I think just tonight showed how fun women's basketball is," Clark said in the postgame conference. "Two really great teams that went at it. I'm sure so many people wish this was a series of seven games. That would be really, really fun."[4]

CAITLIN CLARK

Coming out of West Des Moines, Iowa, Caitlin Clark captivated basketball fans and nonfans alike with her ability to make shots from nearly anywhere on the court. She stayed in her home state to go to the University of Iowa and helped transform the basketball program into a national power. Since Clark and Reese played against each other in the Final Four and were in the same WNBA Draft, the two players are often mentioned together. Clark led the Hawkeyes to two Final Fours before becoming the number one overall draft pick for the Indiana Fever in 2024.

THE BIG GAME

The showdown between Reese and Clark was set for Sunday, April 2. Two of the best and most famous players in the NCAA would get a chance to face off. This was the biggest game between them, and the world would be watching.

The game did not disappoint. The teams played in front of a massive crowd of cheering fans at the American Airlines Center, including basketball greats such as Sheryl Swoopes and Pau Gasol. LSU's Jasmine Carson had the best game of her collegiate career.

Reese and Clark's rivalry became one of the most prominent in women's basketball.

She scored 22 points off the bench, including a buzzer-beater as time expired in the first half.

Reese put up an impressive performance herself. She had another double-double, scoring 15 points and grabbing ten rebounds. She and Carson were among the five Tigers who scored in double figures that afternoon.

Although Clark scored 30 points, including eight three-pointers, the Hawkeyes were outmatched. They didn't have the defense to stop LSU, and the Tigers won 102–85. For Reese, winning the NCAA title was the biggest moment yet in a basketball career that would make waves on and off the court.

CHAPTER TWO

EARLY YEARS

Angel Reese was born on May 6, 2002, and her parents did not look far for a name for their baby daughter. They named her after her mother, Angel. The name isn't the only thing Angel and her mother share. They are also both tall and love basketball.

Angel Webb Reese, Angel's mother, played basketball for the University of Maryland, Baltimore County (UMBC) from 1988 to 1992. In 2025 she still ranked fifth in all-time points for the Retrievers as well as third in rebounds and second in blocks.[1] She was inducted into the UMBC Athletic Hall of Fame.

She went on to play professionally for one year for a team in Luxembourg. Angel's father, Michael, also played basketball at a high level. He played for Boston College and Loyola University Maryland and then also played professionally overseas.

Angel Webb Reese, *right*, has supported her daughter's basketball career from the beginning. >>

One year and one month after Angel's birth, her brother, Julian, was born. Angel's parents divorced when she and her brother were young. Angel grew up in Randallstown, Maryland, and spent a lot of time with her grandparents, Barbara and Curtis Webb.

Her grandparents helped make sure Angel and her brother didn't miss out on anything. "They helped me with Angel and Julian and helping them get to where they are. And to this day, they're very supportive," Angel's mother later recalled. "I think without them, it would've . . . made it a more difficult road to travel."[2]

BASKETBALL FAMILIES

Angel Reese is one of many basketball stars for whom the sport runs in the family. National Basketball Association (NBA) star LeBron James made history in 2024 when he played in an NBA game alongside his son, Bronny. Pamela McGee won an Olympic gold medal and two NCAA titles before playing in the WNBA. Her son, JaVale McGee, won an Olympic gold medal and played for 16 seasons in the NBA, and her daughter, Imani McGee-Stafford, played in the WNBA for three seasons before stepping away to earn a law degree. Dell Curry played for 16 years in the NBA. His sons, Seth and Steph Curry, both have had long NBA careers. Steph is a four-time NBA champion and a two-time Most Valuable Player (MVP).

FINDING HER SPORT

Angel did several sports and activities as a child. She tried softball, volleyball, gymnastics, ballet, cheerleading,

Julian Reese, *left*, attended Angel's twenty-first birthday party on May 6, 2023.

and track. She quickly learned that track was not right for her; she quit a long-distance race before it was over.

But it was basketball that had Angel's heart. It wasn't just her sport. In addition to her parents, her grandfather and aunts played basketball, as did Julian. Her mom continued to play in recreational leagues and coached youth teams. Angel would tag along with her mother and digest everything she could about the game.

Growing up, Angel played basketball at the Scotts Branch Recreation Activity Center. In 2023, a court at the center was dedicated to her.

Her mother remembered this while talking on her daughter's podcast, *Unapologetically Angel*. She said, "I remember you dribbling around the court when I coached. You weren't old enough to play yet. And I would drag you to practice with me and you would be on the sidelines just bouncing the ball and just watching."[3]

Angel's mother figured her daughter would inherit her height—Angel Webb Reese is about six feet (1.8 m) tall. She also thought the young Angel would absorb some of her basketball knowledge. But she saw when her daughter was quite young that Angel could be a great basketball player due to another trait.

"I knew you always had a competitive edge in you," she told Angel on the podcast. "And so no matter what I put you in, you were gonna give it your best. And basketball was a competitive sport. It was a team sport and you worked well with others. . . . I knew at an early age, like around five years old, I was like, 'Yeah, I think she might have it.'"[4]

JULIAN REESE

Angel Reese's brother followed in her footsteps to play basketball at the collegiate level. Julian went to Maryland and has stood out in the Big Ten Conference. Like his sister, Julian is known for posting double-doubles. In 2025, he led the Terrapins to the Sweet 16 of the men's NCAA basketball tournament.

A COMPETITIVE SPIRIT

Angel's competitive edge was honed at home when she and Julian would play against each other, sharpening each other's games. "Everything was just competitive," Angel said. "Our basketball court in front of the house had to be taken away because we were just so competitive. Everything was just always *win, win, and win*. My younger brother didn't want me to be better than him. We used to argue and say, 'Who is taking the shots?' But it really helped my game," Angel said.[5]

Like most siblings, Angel and her brother would argue. It might be about who got to sit in the front seat or which fast-food place to go to. It might be about basketball.

"But at the end of the day," Angel's mom told her on the podcast, "he rides for you, and you ride for him."[6] According to her mother, Angel was a headstrong kid, even stubborn at times. But she also said that Angel was a responsible child and that she could be counted on.

Angel picked up as much as she could about basketball from her mother and brother. She also looked to the professionals for inspiration. She and her mother would go see basketball games whenever they could, often traveling to Washington, DC, to see the Mystics play in the WNBA.

In 2011 Angel met Minnesota Lynx player, four-time WNBA champion, and LSU legend Seimone Augustus. They took a picture together, which Angel shared years later on social media. The picture ended up foreshadowing Angel's future wearing LSU's purple and gold.

Being a single mother was not easy for Webb Reese, and she wanted to give her children everything they needed. She often found strength in Angel and Julian. "As a single parent, I knew that I was gonna have to make sacrifices, but one thing I tell a lot of people is that having you and your brother gave me the strength that I needed to become a stronger person," Webb Reese told her daughter on the podcast. "And because of that strength, it allowed me to support you all in the way that I needed to. And in a way that was best for you all. I did make a lot of sacrifices, but they were well worth it."[7]

Angel first joined the same recreational league that her mother had played in as a child. When it was time for her to face tougher competition, Angel joined Team Takeover, an Amateur Athletic Union (AAU) program. Top AAU teams often travel around to compete against the best teams in the United States.

Seimone Augustus played for the Minnesota Lynx for 14 years.

The AAU has organized girls' basketball teams since 1923.

To raise money to travel to games and tournaments, Angel and her teammates had to get creative. They would "tag," meaning they would stand on street corners in their community and hold cans to collect money. Although Angel didn't like tagging, she and her mother found it was a way to let the community support them. Angel didn't realize how expensive it was for her to be in AAU until she was older, and her mother said that was by design.

"The kids, you all weren't supposed to realize how expensive it was," Webb Reese told Angel. "And that was the purpose of us, the adults. We didn't want you all to be burdened or stressed out. So we took that burden on and man, it was a burden. And it was stressful, but there were some fun days."[8]

The sacrifices ended up being worth it. Angel's early days of basketball were the building blocks for her future in the sport. In high school, she took the next steps to becoming a basketball star.

AMATEUR ATHLETIC UNION

Founded in 1888 by James Sullivan and William Buckingham Curtis, the Amateur Athletic Union (AAU) gives young athletes from the United States a variety of sports opportunities. It is guided by the motto "Sports for All, Forever." The AAU now offers programs in 35 sports, including basketball, and helped Angel Reese get her start in hoops.

CHAPTER THREE

HIGH SCHOOL AND RECRUITING

The next step in Angel's march toward WNBA superstardom was high school. She chose to attend Saint Frances Academy, a school in Baltimore with a history of serving Black students. The school already had a tradition of excellence in basketball, and Angel helped raise its profile even more. The program counted WNBA star and two-time Olympic gold medalist Angel McCoughtry among its alumni. Nia Clouden, a future WNBA first-round draft pick, was playing at Saint Frances when Angel arrived.

Angel quickly made a name for herself on the court. She was a four-year starter for the Panthers. Even in her freshman year, Angel averaged a

Saint Frances Academy is located northeast of downtown Baltimore. >>

double-double, recording 11.1 points and 11 rebounds per game. She was named to the *Baltimore Sun*'s All-Metro first team, a list of the region's top players.

Angel's sophomore year followed a similar script. She was again one of the best girls' basketball players in the Baltimore area, and she was again honored by the *Baltimore Sun*. In both of her first two seasons, the Panthers won the Interscholastic Athletic Association of Maryland (IAAM) A Conference championship.

Though basketball was important, Angel also had interests away from the court. The height that served her so well in basketball was also an asset in volleyball. Angel played for the Saint Frances volleyball team. Her team won conference titles in her freshman and sophomore years.

ST. FRANCES ACADEMY

In 1828, a woman named Elizabeth Clarisse Lange started a school in Maryland with the mission of teaching Black children to read the Bible. This was 37 years before the Thirteenth Amendment ended slavery in the United States. The school continued to serve Black families, including Angel's, and eventually expanded to also welcome boys, including Angel's brother, Julian. Saint Frances Academy is the oldest continuously operating Catholic high school that serves predominantly Black families in the United States.

Academics were also important to Angel. She gave a speech as a senior at Saint Frances discussing why she appreciated the school and how she valued her studies. "When I came [to Saint Frances] as a freshman, I had so much to learn. We have small classes, and many opportunities for individual assistance when needed. The teachers are very interested in each student. Therefore, I became eager to learn and determined to become a scholar and student-athlete at the same time," Angel said, going on to mention that she had a 3.5 or better grade-point average throughout her years at Saint Frances.[1]

Angel's junior basketball season started with her making a bad decision in a scrimmage with a team from Long Reach High School in nearby Columbia, Maryland. She started a fight with an opposing player by punching her. Angel was suspended for three games by her school and had to apologize in front of the student body.

Putting the fight behind her, Angel had a remarkable

In 2018, Reese tried out for the USA Basketball Under-17 team but did not make the team after becoming a finalist.

junior year. She averaged 22.6 points and 19.3 rebounds per game, and the Panthers once again took the IAAM A Conference championship. *The Baltimore Sun* named Angel the All-Metro Girls Basketball Player of the Year.

Her coach at Saint Frances, Jerome Shelton, said at the time he was most impressed with the way Angel had grown as an athlete with the Panthers. "I think the biggest improvement was her decision-making," Shelton said. "She handled pressure situations very well. She's prepared herself mentally in those situations to really play at that [high] level. I see her continuing to climb."[2]

ATTENTION FROM RECRUITERS

Colleges began to show interest in Angel before she even started high school, but recruitment stepped up a notch in the summer before her senior year. While she balanced

NCAA RECRUITMENT

Colleges compete for the best student athletes in a process known as recruitment. In recruiting, college coaches approach student athletes such as Angel to get a feel for what they are like and what their goals are. Coaches then can try to persuade a student athlete to select their college. It's a long process that can start as early as eighth grade, but the NCAA has rules about how contact can be made.

Jerome Shelton was Angel's coach at Saint Frances for the entirety of her high school career.

training with working at summer basketball camps and at a burger shop, she also began to think about her plans for life after high school.

At the time, she wanted to find a school with a strong journalism program, as Angel hoped to start a career in broadcast journalism after her basketball days were over. Angel also wanted a family-like atmosphere, which she was familiar with both at Saint Frances and with Team Takeover, her AAU team. But she also wanted to find a team that could help her excel on the court. "I want to be able to play my position, grabbing a rebound and taking off on the dribble," Angel said.[3]

ESPN ranked Angel as the number two college prospect in the country behind Paige Bueckers, who would go on to play for the University of Connecticut. Angel had many schools interested in her. She narrowed her list to the University of Maryland, the University of South Carolina, the University of Southern California, Syracuse University, and the University of Tennessee. She scheduled visits to Maryland and Tennessee in early September of her senior year.

College Park, Maryland, the home of the University of Maryland, is about an hour's drive from Randallstown. The school won a national championship in women's basketball in 2006. With Brenda Frese as the head coach, the school attracted several top players who went on to succeed in the WNBA, including Alyssa Thomas and Kristi Toliver. With Angel growing up in Maryland, Frese started recruiting her in eighth grade.

In early November, Angel announced she would stick close to home and try to bring a national championship to the state she was born and raised in. She praised the College Park campus and Frese's program. "Each time I visit, it feels like home even more," she said. "I love the coaches and players. I can academically be successful at Maryland while studying my major of journalism. I think

Reese was excited to attend the University of Maryland and expected it to a be good fit for her academically and athletically.

they have the tools to win a national championship and I want to bring that home to my home state."[4]

FINISHING UP AT HIGH SCHOOL

With college recruitment over, Angel could focus on her senior year of high school. She once again led the Panthers to an IAAM championship. Saint Frances retired her number 10 jersey, making her the first female athlete to earn that honor at her school. The *Baltimore Sun* named her the All-Metro Basketball Player of the Year and also the High School Female Athlete of the Year.

An ugly incident, though, cast a shadow over the conclusion of her high school career. A popular Instagram account that focused on women's basketball posted

McDONALD'S ALL-AMERICAN GAME

Started in 1977, the McDonald's All-American Game has showcased some of the best high school senior basketball players in the United States and Canada, with a girls' game added in 2002. Being chosen to play in the game is one of the biggest honors in high school hoops. The All-Americans play in an exhibition game, dunk contest, and three-point contest. They also participate in charity events such as a visit to a local Ronald McDonald house. Angel Reese was on the roster with her future WNBA teammate Kamilla Cardoso. Stars including Michael Jordan, Kobe Bryant, and Candace Parker were McDonald's All-Americans before they hit the big time.

a highlight video featuring Angel. Lisa Smith, a coach from rival Archbishop Spalding High School in Severn, Maryland, replied privately to criticize Angel. The coach said Angel had "zero humility or impulse control" and asserted that "you can have swag while not acting like a punk."[5]

The message upset Angel. "That's a team that I played against for four years, and we just played them last week and I never had a problem with them," Angel said. "It's hurtful that someone would come at me in that way. I never try to hurt anyone. I just play hard."[6]

Smith apologized to Angel and her family, but Angel was still upset. The situation foreshadowed the kind of criticism that she would receive as her fame continued to grow. Smith lost her job as the coach at Archbishop Spalding due to her statements.

Angel was named to the McDonald's All-American Game, an event that is intended to showcase the best in high school basketball and give athletes special events in their final days of high school. Unfortunately, the COVID-19 pandemic, which spread in early 2020, led to the cancellation of the game. Now, only summer break stood between Angel and the beginning of her college basketball career.

CHAPTER FOUR

MARYLAND TERRAPIN

When Reese started her freshman year at Maryland, she was a new member of a team with several older, more experienced players. But she was used to being a vocal leader on the court, and she didn't change that just because she was in a new place. She cheered on her teammates just as loudly in practice as she had when she was at Saint Frances or with Team Takeover.

"It hasn't been unusual for me because it started like that when I was in high school," Reese said before her freshman season began. "I am the baby on the team, but I knew that I had to bring something different from everybody. My communication

Reese brought her number 10 to the Maryland Terrapins. >>

B1G
10

throughout practice, my leadership throughout practice, picking up teammates if they miss a shot, just always being there for my teammates, I know I can always bring that every day even if I don't have the best game."[1]

The year before Reese arrived, the Terrapins went 28–4 in the 2019–2020 season. The NCAA Tournament was canceled due to COVID-19, so the team didn't get the chance to demonstrate their skills in March Madness. Then, before the 2020–2021 season, two starters, Shakira Austin and Taylor Mikesell, transferred to other schools. But with top recruit Reese and returning players Diamond Miller and Ashley Owusu, Terrapin fans were excited to see what this team could accomplish.

WHAT IS A TERRAPIN?

The University of Maryland had a unique mascot cheering on Reese when she played there. The diamondback terrapin is a type of turtle that is native to the Chesapeake Bay. It is known for the beautiful patterns on its shell. The terrapin has not always been Maryland's mascot. In the early 1900s, the school's teams were variously called the Old Liners, Farmers, or Aggies. In 1933, the university's vice president wrote to a seafood company to ask for a terrapin to be used as the model for the school's new mascot. The nickname stuck, and Maryland teams have been called Terrapins, or Terps for short, ever since.

After her foot injury during the Towson game, Reese needed crutches to support herself.

Unfortunately for Reese, her season was marred early by an injury. In a game on December 3 against Towson, she broke her foot and had to sit out for 12 weeks. While Reese was out, her teammates put up a record of 13–1.

On February 23, 2021, the Terrapins welcomed the Iowa Hawkeyes to the Xfinity Center on the College Park campus. Iowa was led by the freshman phenomenon Clark, an opponent Reese would come to know well. The game turned out to be one for the record books.

In a raucous environment, Maryland's Katie Benzan tied and then broke a Maryland record for three-pointers, going nine-for-ten from behind the arc. Three Maryland players scored more than 20 points. Although Clark scored 34, the Hawkeyes couldn't stop the Terrapins. Maryland won the game 111–93.

Reese came off the bench, playing 13 minutes for the first time since December. She scored eight points and grabbed three rebounds. It wasn't her best performance, but her team was happy she was back.

"She's 100 percent healed. We wanted to test the waters if it presented itself today," Frese said after the game. "We're not going to be able to practice tomorrow after this physical game. I thought she was huge. I thought her energy was great, to be able to have that energy and depth and to be able to send waves."[2]

BRENDA FRESE

Reese's first coach in college was Maryland's Brenda Frese. She has been the head coach for Maryland since 2002. Her coaching life began while she was still in college at the University of Arizona. After an injury, she spent time as a volunteer coach at a nearby community college. She continued to coach at different schools until Maryland hired her. By 2025, Frese had guided the Terrapins to one national championship and three Final Fours.

BACK TO THE GAME

Maryland's winning season continued. The team won out the rest of the regular season and then took the Big Ten

Tournament title. The championship game was a rematch with Iowa. Clark put up 21 points, shooting four-for-ten from the three-point line. For the Terrapins, Chloe Bibby matched Clark's score of 21 points.

Reese's minutes were again limited, but she was able to celebrate a 104–84 win with her team. Maryland earned a guaranteed spot in the NCAA Tournament. The NCAA committee gave the Terrapins a two seed, meaning they would have an easier road to the Final Four than most of the teams in the tournament.

Usually, the first two rounds of the women's NCAA Tournament are played on the campuses of the top-seeded schools. The winners then travel to regional sites before heading to the Final Four. But this was in 2021, when many COVID-19 restrictions were still in place. The NCAA decided to play every game in San Antonio, Texas, the city that had originally been awarded the Final Four. Most games were played at the Alamodome. A small number of fans, friends, and family were allowed to attend the games.

The Terrapins cruised to wins in their first two games. Maryland's first game was against Mount Saint Mary's University, a 15 seed. The Terps' defense stopped the Mount Saint Mary's scoring attack effectively.

Reese made eight of her 12 attempted shots during Maryland's second-round game against Alabama.

Meanwhile, five Maryland players scored in the double digits. Frese continued to be careful with Reese as she returned from her injury. She played ten minutes and scored 11 points, helping her team to a 98–45 win.

In the second round, Maryland scored 100 points on the University of Alabama. Reese had her best game yet since her injury. Coming off the bench, she had 19 points, two assists, five rebounds, and one block. The Terrapins had made it to the Sweet 16.

Next, Maryland faced the University of Texas Longhorns. Seeded sixth, the Longhorns had defeated three-seed University of California, Los Angeles (UCLA) in the second round and were playing close to their hometown of Austin, Texas. The Longhorns limited the Terps' high-scoring offense to only 61 points. Reese played nine minutes but didn't score any points. Texas pulled the upset 64–61, sending Maryland back to College Park.

NEXT SEASON

The loss was painful, but Maryland still had plenty to look forward to in the next year. Miller was only a sophomore, and Reese was a freshman who was still getting back to full strength. Owusu and Benzan would be back too. They would have more time to play together and potentially record some big wins for the school.

But first, Reese had to find herself on the court again. The injury that kept her out for 14 games in her freshman season had not just hurt her physically. It took a bite out of her confidence, making her question herself on the court. The foot fracture had come on a simple layup, a move she had made hundreds of times in her basketball career. She had to find a way to make that layup again without thinking about the injury.

"For anybody who has had an injury, you doubt yourself," Reese said early in the 2021–2022 season.

You try to not think about that stuff, but it's natural as a human being to think, "Will I ever be the same?"

You look at others, and you just think, "Why me? Why did I have to go through this? How come no one else did?" But then I got to thinking, "The only one that can stop me is myself. I can't control what others do. I can only control what I do." I just knew that if I worked hard in rehab and did everything I could do, I could get back to where I was before.[3]

Part of her journey included journaling, meditating, and controlling her social media usage. When she was on the bench and couldn't play at Maryland, she focused on being a positive presence for her team. Another part of the journey was keeping her basketball skills sharp.

After the 2020–2021 season ended in disappointment, she found other ways to get on the court. Reese tried out for the USA Basketball Under-19 team, making it to the final round of roster cuts. She also helped Maryland earn a silver medal in the 3x Nationals, a three-on-three basketball tournament.

This all led to Reese starting the 2021–2022 season with high expectations. The team was ranked fourth in the preseason Associated Press (AP) poll of the top 25 teams. Maryland won its first six games, including a 79–76 win over Baylor University, ranked number six. The Terps then traveled to the Bahamas for a set of games against some

Reese said that she enjoyed the fast pace of three-on-three basketball.

of the best teams in the United States. Maryland lost to North Carolina State University and then to Stanford University, and its ranking dropped from second to eighth.

From there, the Terrapins' season proceeded like it was on a roller coaster. Although the Terrapins played well against most teams, ranked programs gave them more trouble. They lost games to number one South Carolina, number eight Indiana, number 11 University of Michigan, and number 25 Ohio State University.

On Valentine's Day in 2022, Maryland once again faced Iowa. Playing at Carver–Hawkeye Arena in Iowa City, Reese had one of her best games of the season. She scored 25 points, pulled down 13 rebounds, and blocked two shots. The Terrapins won 81–69.

But Maryland could not roll the late-season momentum into the Big Ten Tournament. The team lost to Indiana in the first round. The Hoosiers' defense was effective, and Reese was the only Maryland starter who scored more than four points.

TRANSFER PORTAL

If an athlete such as Reese wants to switch schools, she puts her name into the transfer portal. This database coordinates and tracks which players are available to transfer. The athletes can indicate whether they want coaches to contact them. Since 2022, athletes have been able to transfer schools without losing any eligibility. Previously, athletes needed to sit out a year if they transferred schools, and the original school would first need to approve the transfer.

Still, Maryland earned a number four seed in the NCAA Tournament. The school hosted games at the Xfinity Center on the College Park campus. In the first round, Maryland faced a nearby foe, the University of Delaware Blue Hens. Every Terrapins starter scored in double figures, with Owusu leading the way with 24 points, and Maryland won 102–71.

In the second round, the Terrapins had a tougher test in Florida Gulf Coast University, a team that had been ranked much of the season. Both Miller and Reese had spectacular games, scoring 24 and 21 points, respectively, and Maryland won 89–65. Once again, the Terrapins made it to the Sweet 16.

But their road would end there. Facing Stanford in a regional matchup in Spokane, Washington, Maryland could not overcome the defending champion. Despite Reese's 25 points, nine rebounds, and three blocks, Maryland lost 72–66. Once again, a promising season ended in disappointment.

Maryland would not get a chance to try again the next season with the same players. At the end of March, five Terrapin players entered the transfer portal, an NCAA database of players looking to switch schools. The biggest star in that group was Reese. She was on the lookout for a new school and a new place to play basketball.

By April, Reese had decided that she would transfer to Louisiana State University (LSU). She wanted a fresh start for her basketball career. For the first time, she was moving far away from home.

> **“I took the scariest step of my life! I had to bet on myself & stand firm on what I wanted for myself! TAKE THE STEP THAT MAKES YOU HAPPY!!!”**[4]
>
> **—Angel Reese in a social media post on her decision to transfer to LSU**

CHAPTER FIVE

LOUISIANA STATE TIGER

Coach Kim Mulkey's success at Baylor was unquestionable. She led the Bears to three national championships, and she sent several players, including superstar Brittney Griner, to the WNBA. There weren't many places that would make her consider leaving the university's Texas home. She wasn't a Texan—she grew up in Louisiana and played basketball at Louisiana Tech in the early days of NCAA women's hoops—but she had built a good life there.

In late April 2021, LSU announced its head coach, Nikki Fargas, had resigned. LSU needed a new head coach. LSU athletic director Scott Woodward reached

Kim Mulkey's eye-catching outfits make her a striking presence on the sideline during LSU games. >>

WIN

out to Mulkey. Just days after Fargas resigned, Mulkey was announced as the school's new head coach.

At her opening press conference, Mulkey promised her team would win a national championship but also asked for patience. "Understand that it will not happen overnight. I'm going to repeat that over and over. There's a lot of things to do, and we'll do it as quickly as we can, but we won't do any shortcuts," she said.[1]

Playing with a team composed mostly of athletes Fargas had recruited, the Tigers did well in Mulkey's first season. They went 26–6 and reached the second round of the NCAA Tournament. It was a good start, but it wasn't the national championship that Mulkey had promised.

ANGEL ARRIVES

After entering the transfer portal, Reese made an official visit to LSU's campus in Baton Rouge, Louisiana.

KIM MULKEY'S DAYS AS A PLAYER

Long before Kim Mulkey became Reese's coach, she was a standout player herself. Playing for Hall of Fame coach Sonja Hogg, Mulkey was the small and feisty point guard who helped Louisiana Tech University win the first NCAA women's basketball title in 1982. Then, in 1984, Mulkey helped Team USA win gold at the Los Angeles Olympics.

She was joined by her friend Kateri Poole, who was also considering transferring to LSU. Both were impressed with Baton Rouge and LSU. At a team dinner at Mulkey's house, Reese and Poole agreed that they would transfer to the school.

On May 6, 2022, LSU announced that Reese was now a Tiger. "Angel is coming to Baton Rouge as one of the most dynamic players in the country," Mulkey said in a press release. "She's an outstanding scorer with a knack for rebounding that will make an immediate impact in our frontcourt. I'm excited to get Angel on campus this summer and get to work!"[2]

Reese's comments were just as enthusiastic. "I chose LSU and Kim Mulkey because of the winning culture," she added in the press release. "I trust in Coach Kim and her staff to help develop me into the player I need to be for the next level. Her résumé speaks for itself and I want to continue that here at LSU.

Reese often plays with her left leg covered to hide a surgery scar on her shin.

The relationships I've built here, especially with the team are so special and we are ready to work! Let's Geaux Tigers!"[3]

MIKE THE TIGER

While at LSU, Reese could visit a real live tiger. Mike the Tiger, LSU's mascot, lives in a lush habitat on campus. In 2005, a new habitat was built containing a stream, rocky terrain, and plenty of trees. Fans who cannot visit Baton Rouge in person can keep an eye on Mike virtually via a webcam.

Reese wasn't the only star headed to Baton Rouge. Flau'jae Johnson, a freshman from Savannah, Georgia, was a talented rapper and a point guard. She announced her commitment to LSU with the release of a music video. There were other promising players on the team, including Alexis Morris and LaDazhia Williams.

Before the season, Mulkey again emphasized that the team had a lot of work to do before a national championship would be possible. "We have a lot of talent on the floor. We've got to piece it together," she said. "We've got kids coming from other programs, high school kids stepping on college campus for the first time, returning players who have to play different roles. It takes time."[4]

The reporters covering women's basketball agreed. LSU was predicted to finish third in the SEC and was ranked sixteenth overall in the AP preseason national poll.

South Carolina, the defending national champions and a conference rival for LSU, was ranked first.

The only way for the Tigers to prove they were a better team this year was to win, and that's just what they did at the start of the 2022–2023 season. LSU won its first five games of the season, scoring at least 100 points in all of them. In mid-November, Reese was named the SEC Co-Player of the Week, and Johnson was honored by the conference as the Freshman of the Week. Reese earned the honor again just two weeks later; she had recorded a double-double in every game so far that season.

November went by without a loss for the Tigers. December was more of the same. Reese continued to register double-doubles. In a December game in Hawaii against Oregon State University, she scored 25 points and grabbed 20 rebounds. She passed the 1,000-point mark in this game, an especially impressive feat given that she had missed most of her freshman season.[5]

Reese's contributions weren't just on the court. Her teammates said she brought the exact kind of leadership the team needed to find its identity and win. "She's what I hoped for times 50," Morris said in late December. "She's amazing. She's the best teammate I've played with in college, on and off the floor. She's the glue to the

Mulkey praised Reese's passion for basketball and her ability to pull down offensive rebounds.

team with her energy on both ends of the floor and off the court."[6]

Most of the teams that LSU faced in the first couple of months of the season weren't very tough competition. Only one team, Oregon State, came from one of the Power Five conferences, the most prominent conferences in college sports. None were ranked in the AP top 25.

Although LSU had an undefeated record, it was hard to tell just how good the Tigers were. When asked, Mulkey said, "I don't know how good we are either. I do know we have talent. We've handled our schedule pretty darned well."[7]

The first real test came on December 29. The Tigers traveled to Fayetteville, Arkansas, to face the ranked-twenty-fourth University of Arkansas Razorbacks in their first conference matchup of the season. LSU's wins to that point had been marked by outstanding offense.

This game, though, showed what LSU could do on the other end of the court. The defense held Arkansas to 27 percent shooting from the field. Meanwhile, both Morris and Reese scored 19 points on the way to a 69–45 win. With it, the team jumped to number seven in the AP poll.

The winning continued as 2023 began. The Tigers climbed to number three in the AP poll just in time for a showdown with South Carolina. Coached by Dawn Staley, a three-time Olympic gold medalist and five-time WNBA

In LSU's game against South Carolina, Reese made only five of her attempted 15 field goals.

All-Star in her playing days, the Gamecocks had a loaded starting lineup and a deep bench of talented players to dominate the NCAA.

Both teams were undefeated when LSU showed up to play at Colonial Life Arena in Columbia, South Carolina. Playing in front of a large crowd, South Carolina took an early lead. Mulkey called a time-out a minute into the game after the Gamecocks' quick 6–0 start.

The Gamecocks were led by Kamilla Cardoso, who was coming off the bench. She used her 6-foot-7 frame to control the court. Another major contributor was Aliyah Boston, who had won the 2022 Wooden Award as the national player of the year.

South Carolina won the battle of rebounding, with Reese grabbing only four. It was the first time all season she didn't get a double-double. South Carolina won the game 88–64. It was a wake-up call for LSU with the postseason looming.

Reese was drawing attention for her abilities and emotion on the court. She would trash-talk, sometimes to the point of being penalized. In games against Arkansas and Florida, she drew technical fouls. Mulkey said she didn't want to ever take Reese's passion away from her, and Reese agreed that it's an important part of her game.

Reese is known for being a vocal player on the court.

"I feel like that's what separates me from a lot of players, that I have that dog mentality and I always want to go out there and win and I'm very passionate about that," she said. "So whoever's in front of me, I'm going to go get it, and I'm going to talk trash to you the whole entire game, and that's that."[8]

She was also getting noticed for how she managed to stay glamorous even while playing her game. She said before the season started that making sure her hair and makeup looked just right was part of her pregame routine. "Grandma would always emphasize, 'Don't let anybody make your makeup sweat,'" Reese said.[9] Her look, her social media presence, and of course her skills on the

Reese's trash-talking celebration after LSU's win over Iowa became a viral moment.

court meant that Reese could score lucrative deals with companies such as Amazon and Xfinity.

With more of a spotlight on her than ever before, Reese and the Tigers shifted their focus to the postseason. First, they would have to play in the SEC tournament. As the number one and number two seeds, South Carolina and LSU were on opposite sides of the bracket. If form held, LSU would get a rematch with South Carolina in the tournament final.

After an easy win over Georgia, LSU faced Tennessee in the semifinals. The Tigers took an early lead, but

Rickea Jackson and Jordan Horston led the Lady Vols back for a 69–67 win. Angel recorded her twenty-eighth double-double of the season, breaking the LSU record that had been held by legend Sylvia Fowles.

The Tigers didn't have time to sulk over the upset loss, though. Just two weeks later, they would host the first two rounds of the NCAA Tournament, with Michigan and Hawaii coming to Baton Rouge for games. This time, the Tigers found their stride. They rolled past Hawaii and Michigan and outlasted Utah in the Sweet 16.

After topping upset-minded Miami in the Elite Eight, they clamped down high-powered Virginia Tech in the Final Four. That set up the dramatic showdown against Caitlin Clark and Iowa. Reese and the Tigers prevailed for the school's first-ever national title.

> **"All year, I was critiqued about who I was. . . . I don't fit in the box that y'all want me to be in. I'm too hood. I'm too ghetto. . . . But when other people do it, y'all don't say nothing. So this was for the girls that look like me, that's going to speak up on what they believe in. It's unapologetically you."** [10]
>
> **—Angel Reese, after winning the 2023 NCAA women's basketball championship**

With the win, Reese became a national celebrity. She was also at the center of controversy. In the final minutes of the win over Iowa, Reese celebrated by staring at Clark and waving her hand in front of her own face, pointing to where her championship ring would go. It was a taunt that Clark had also done in a previous game. With the game drawing a record number of viewers, many people who didn't normally watch women's basketball, and thus weren't familiar with the sport's norms surrounding trash talk, criticized Reese. The word "classless" trended on social media as people discussed the controversial moment.

But Reese would not be intimidated. She posted a picture on social media of her doing the gesture in the game. Clark defended Reese's actions, pointing out that trash talk is a part of basketball.

"I don't think Angel should be criticized at all. I'm just one that competes, and she competed," Clark said. "I think everybody knew there was going to be a little trash talk in the entire tournament. It's not just me and Angel. We're all competitive. We all show our emotions in a different way."[11]

POSTSEASON PLAY

With the season over, Reese had some off-the-court recognition come her way. Reese was featured in the 2023 *Time* 100 Next list of emerging leaders. In the feature,

Candace Parker wrote that Reese was "ripping the sport open and tearing back the layers."[12]

Before long, it was time for LSU to start focusing on the next season. Once again, Mulkey was successful with the transfer portal. The Tigers landed Aneesah Morrow, a scoring machine from Chicago, Illinois, who had played her first two years at DePaul University, and Hailey Van Lith, a guard who had led the University of Louisville to the Final Four in 2022.

LSU hadn't lost many players to graduation. The team was also adding a top-rated recruiting class. The Tigers were poised to be unstoppable in Reese's senior season.

The hype around LSU at the beginning of the season was huge. Four players, including Reese, were named to preseason All-SEC teams. LSU was ranked number one in the nation in the first AP poll. After Shaquille O'Neal,

NAME, IMAGE, AND LIKENESS

Starting in July 2021, student athletes playing sports at NCAA schools were allowed to profit off their name, image, and likeness (NIL). This meant that college athletes could get paid for endorsements and advertisements the way professional athletes can. Some athletes might make just a few hundred dollars a year, but top stars such as Reese can sign deals worth millions of dollars.

another LSU legend, became Reebok's president of basketball operations, he signed Reese to the brand.

But the beginning of the season was bumpy for the Tigers. They lost their first game 92–78 to Colorado. Then, during LSU's game against Kent State on November 14, Reese was pulled from the game at halftime. Mulkey wouldn't answer questions about the benching. "I could, but I won't. It was just a coach's decision," Mulkey said.[13]

Reese missed the next four games. Mulkey continued to be cagey about her star player's absence. Reese didn't address the media during her time away from her team, but she posted on social media, "Please don't believe everything you read."[14]

She returned for the Tigers' November 30 game, a repeat of the Final Four matchup against Virginia Tech. The Tigers again prevailed, with four players scoring in the double digits. After the win, Reese called her absence a reset for her mental health. "My mental health is the most important thing before anything, and I'm gonna make sure I'm ok before anything," she explained.[15]

The rest of the nonconference season was much like the previous one. The Tigers didn't lose, but they also didn't face tough competition. The conference part of the season started with LSU winning as well. But then the

Reese pulled down an outstanding total of 19 rebounds during LSU's first-round game against Rice University in the 2024 NCAA Tournament.

Tigers began to lose games. The team had plenty of great players, but they lacked chemistry.

LSU was ranked only eighth by the time the SEC tournament rolled around, a far cry from the number one ranking at the beginning of the season. The Tigers won a rematch against Auburn and then won against the University of Mississippi to get to the conference championship against South Carolina. Once again, South Carolina won, this time with a final score of 79–72. Reese notched a double-double, but it wasn't enough.

After LSU's loss to Iowa, Reese and her teammates answered questions from the media in a press conference.

For the NCAA Tournament, LSU was given a three seed. The Tigers hosted teams at the Pete Maravich Athletic Center in Baton Rouge. They beat Rice University in the opening round. Middle Tennessee State University knocked out the higher-seeded University of Louisville in the first round, and then LSU turned around and defeated Middle Tennessee State. Playing in the Sweet 16 in Albany, New York, the Tigers won 78–69 over UCLA. This set the stage for a rematch against Iowa, with the winning team moving ahead to the Final Four.

This time, the game was Iowa's. LSU didn't have the defense to stop Clark, who scored 41 points. Iowa was able to capitalize on LSU's turnovers and won 94–87. Clark and Reese shared a hug after the game, and Reese cried in the postgame press conference as she talked about the death threats and other difficulties she had dealt with throughout the year. "I don't really get to stand up for myself," she said.

> *I have great teammates. I have a great support system. I've got my hometown. I've got my family that stands up for me. I don't really get to speak out on things just because I just try to ignore. I just try to stand strong . . . I've been through so much, seen so much. I've been attacked so many times.*[16]

Reese still had a year of NCAA eligibility left. Her next decision was the biggest one of her basketball career so far. She needed to decide whether to stay at LSU another year or enter her name in the WNBA Draft.

CHAPTER SIX

THE 2024 WNBA DRAFT

Reese did not have much time to process LSU's loss in the NCAA Tournament. She had to start thinking about her next steps. She could have stayed in college for another year, but after four years of playing collegiate ball, she was eligible to enter her name into the WNBA Draft and have a shot at starting her professional career.

Because the WNBA season starts in early May, the turnaround from the end of the NCAA Tournament to the draft is quick. Reese's last game with LSU was on April 1, 2024, and the draft was on April 15. New professional players then get about a week to pack up their lives in their college towns, move to the cities of

Reese reused the symbol of a crown in promotional images taken during the 2024 WNBA Draft. >>

Reese appeared on the cover of *Vogue* in January 2025.

the teams that drafted them, and prepare for a grueling training camp.

Several of these athletes are still finishing out their classwork in college. These challenges add to the stresses of media and name, image, and likeness (NIL) obligations and the ups and downs of a big life transition. This can make it a tough but thrilling time for the young athletes.

Knowing the whirlwind her life would turn into in March and April, Reese made her decision well before she announced it. In early March, between the SEC tournament and the first round of the NCAA Tournament, she told the fashion magazine *Vogue* that she was heading to the WNBA.

Reese has always been a fan of fashion. She was given the nickname "Bayou Barbie" by LSU fans because of her love of clothes, bags, shoes, long eyelashes, and long hair. Reese was even the subject of a photo spread for *Teen Vogue*.

HISTORY OF THE WNBA

In the spring of 1996, the NBA announced the founding of a women's basketball league, the WNBA. With the popularity of the 1996 gold-medal-winning US women's Olympic team, the league started with eight teams. The first game was played on June 21, 1997, at the Great Western Forum in Los Angeles, California, between the Los Angeles Sparks and the New York Liberty. The league celebrated its twenty-fifth season in 2021. Those first players paved the way for Reese.

When it was time to share her WNBA announcement, Reese looked at what her heroes had done. Serena Williams, another athlete who loved fashion, shared the news of her retirement in *Vogue*, and Reese wanted to follow suit. On April 3, 2024, *Vogue* published the news in an article titled "Angel Reese Is Taking Her Talents to the WNBA."

Reese emphasized that she knew she was going to be starting at the bottom when she got to the WNBA. But she felt a new challenge would help her grow as a player. "I want to start at the bottom again," she said. "I want to be a rookie again and build myself back up; I want to be knocked down and learn and grow at the next level."[1]

LSU would miss Reese's play and the swagger she brought to the team, but her coach, Kim Mulkey, understood; she had prepared players for the WNBA in the past. Mulkey said Reese had "helped transform our program. We are all indebted to Angel Reese for the contributions she has given to this program, helping us win our first national championship, and the contributions she made on our university as a whole."[2]

THE DRAFT

The Elite Eight game between Reese's LSU Tigers and Clark's Iowa Hawkeyes had once again broken viewership ratings records for women's college basketball.[3] The draft that year would be held in New York City. Heading into the event, the WNBA wanted to capture some of the magic from the superstar college players.

Reese was invited to New York City early. She joined Clark, Kamilla Cardoso, Cameron Brink, Rickea Jackson, and other top players who were expected to be draft picks. They visited the top of the Empire State Building, took selfies, and pressed buttons to light the top in orange, the league's color.

These women had been playing one another fiercely in games just weeks before, but they were bonded in

Reese and the draftees who joined her at the top of the Empire State Building wore the WNBA's orange color.

this moment. Reese shared on social media that she loved getting to know the other prospects in a more relaxed environment. She wrote, "The best part of the weekend in NYC was getting to know all the girls after being sooo competitive for the last 4 years!! Everybody was such a vibe & we all had so much FUN which shows how competitive we all are ON THE COURT!! NOTHING IS PERSONAL!!!"[3]

The WNBA prospects used draft night to show off their style. Reese again used her love of fashion to create her look. She understood that the pictures taken on this night would be used for the rest of her career. Figuring out how to present herself was also a way for Reese to connect with her grandmother. "I used to always watch the draft with my grandma, and she was always like, 'Whatchu gonna wear? Whatchu gonna wear? That's gonna be the most important thing!'" Reese said.[4]

Reese wore a silver, hooded, backless, floor-length dress. After one dress didn't fit and another got lost in the mail, this dress was actually her third choice, but it still landed her on best-dressed lists for the night. She paired it with silver heels and a silver bag, creating a dramatic look.

The draft was her next step in making her professional dreams come true. "As a little girl, I always dreamed of that moment, of being able to actually put the dress on for it, and then hearing [WNBA Commissioner] Miss Cathy [Engelbert] call my name," she said as she got ready for the draft that night. "So I'm just taking it all in right now."[5]

"I've done everything I wanted to in college. I've won a national championship, I've gotten SEC Player of the Year, I've been an All-American. My ultimate goal is to be a pro—and to be one of the greatest basketball players to play, ever. I feel like I'm ready."[6]

—Angel Reese, April 2024, declaring that she would enter the WNBA Draft

Reese walked the orange carpet, posing for pictures by herself and with her fellow prospects.

Every prospect joined Engelbert on the stage and then settled in at tables with their loved ones. Reese sat with the people who had supported her throughout her life: her mother, her brother, and her grandparents. Mulkey sat in the audience with other coaches.

The draft started as expected, with Clark going to the Indiana Fever. Next, Brink, from Stanford, went to the Los Angeles Sparks. The Chicago Sky, a team rebuilding just a few years after winning a WNBA championship, picked Cardoso from South Carolina, a player whom Reese had faced several times. The Sky had a new coach in WNBA legend Teresa Weatherspoon, nicknamed "T-Spoon," and she was known for her love of defense.

With the fourth pick, the Sparks selected Jackson from Tennessee. Then the Dallas Wings chose Ohio State's

WNBA COMMISSIONER CATHY ENGELBERT

Before 2019, the WNBA had been led by a president. But that year, Cathy Engelbert was named the league's first commissioner. She came from the world of business, most recently working as the chief executive officer of Deloitte, a consulting firm. After taking charge of the WNBA, she helped create a new collective bargaining agreement between teams and players; signed new, more lucrative television deals; and brought in three new WNBA teams. Her job also includes announcing draft picks such as Reese.

Jacy Sheldon, and the Washington Mystics took UConn's Aaliyah Edwards. The Sky were then up for another pick. Engelbert announced that Chicago was choosing Reese with the seventh pick. Reese shook her head with a smile on her face, then hugged her mother, brother, and grandparents before waving to the LSU group.

As she accepted the Sky jersey from Engelbert, Reese again shook her head while smiling. After posing for pictures, she stopped to talk with ESPN's Holly Rowe. "I'm just so excited. I get to play with Kamilla! I've been playing against her since high school. I'm excited to play with Kamilla, and T-Spoon is amazing. She's done some great things. I'm excited to be coached by her," Reese said, holding back tears. "A kid from Baltimore is not supposed to be here."[7]

The day before the draft, the Sky had traded for the Minnesota Lynx's seventh pick to increase their chances

OTHER SEVENTH PICKS

Angel Reese is in good company among the league's seventh overall draft picks. Other seventh picks include Kahleah Copper, a four-time All-Star and Olympic gold medalist; Ariel Atkins, a two-time All-Star and Olympic gold medalist; and Essence Carson, a champion in the WNBA with a 12-year career in the league.

After being drafted, Engelbert, *right*, gave Reese a jersey bearing the number 24, representing the year the draft took place.

of getting Reese. The Sky had a new general manager, Jeff Pagliocca, and wanted to make the team's draft picks count. In picking Cardoso and Reese, the Sky's frontcourt was instantly upgraded.

"We are absolutely thrilled we were able to get Angel at seventh overall," Pagliocca said on the night of the draft. "That was our hope. We have another incredibly competitive player in Chicago who fits our identity and culture of the city. She is a relentless rebounder, she is a national champion and an SEC Player of the Year and we cannot wait to see her here in Chi Town."[8]

Sky training camp began on April 27, 2025, almost two weeks after the WNBA Draft.

REACHING FOR THE SKY

In 2021, the Sky had added WNBA legend and Chicago native Candace Parker to a team that already had a solid core with All-Stars Courtney Vandersloot, Kahleah Copper, and Allie Quigley. Despite a bad start to the season and a sixth seed in the playoffs, the Sky made an improbable run and won the WNBA championship.

In 2022, despite upgrading their roster by adding Emma Meesseman, a star player from Belgium, the Sky were knocked out of the playoffs in the semifinal round by the Connecticut Sun. After that, Parker and Vandersloot signed with other teams. Quigley stepped away from the game, and Meesseman stayed in Europe to play on the Belgian national team.

In 2023, Sky coach James Wade left midseason for a job in the NBA. Copper asked for a trade after the season. The Sky honored her request and sent her to the Phoenix Mercury.

After such a dramatic rise followed by an equally dramatic fall, Sky fans were hungry for a reason to be excited about the team. Cardoso and Reese fit the bill. Just two days after the draft, Reese made a TikTok video announcing that in addition to being "Baltimore Barbie" and "Bayou Barbie," she was now "Chi Barbie." She thanked the fans for their overwhelming love. Within days, her jersey was sold out online, and ticket sales surged.

Reese's dream of playing in the WNBA had never been closer. "As a little girl, I always looked up to so many great players in the WNBA," she said. "Now, being able to see my name on the back of a jersey is amazing." Reese, though, knew she still had work to do to make the team. She said she wouldn't take the opportunity for granted and vowed to do "whatever it takes, because I don't want my spot taken."[9]

CHAPTER SEVEN

CHICAGO SKY

Just days after the draft, Reese made her way to Chicago with one goal in mind: making the team. In most professional sports leagues, a first-round draft pick would be guaranteed a spot on the team. But in the WNBA, even first-round picks aren't always spared from cuts because of a small number of roster spots.

In 2024, there were 12 teams with 12 roster spots each, meaning a total of just 144 players in the league. Although 36 players had just been drafted, there would not be 36 open spots. Rookies had to go above and beyond to prove they were ready for the league's play, which was faster and much more physical than college basketball.

"I don't want to go into the league thinking that I'm automatically on the team because I'm not," Reese said in her introductory press conference. "Anybody can

In a preseason game against the Minnesota Lynx, Reese scored 13 points for the Sky. Her team lost 92–81. >>

CHICAG
5
Wilson
OFFICIAL
GAME BALL

get cut any given day. We have amazing vets on our team and I know they're gonna push me every day to get even better. There's no given spot. I don't take this moment for granted [as if] I'm just gonna have it given to me. I need to go out there and earn my spot."[1]

While she was balancing training camp and finishing her classes at LSU, Reese was given a special opportunity. After appearing in *Vogue* and *Cosmopolitan*, Reese was invited to the vaunted Met Gala at New York City's Metropolitan Museum of Art. At this fashion and fundraising event, celebrities from various fields show up in extravagant costumes.

Reese couldn't miss practice. But she also knew opportunities like this didn't come along all the time. Stressed about upcoming finals and trying to make the

MET GALA

On the first Monday of May, the Costume Institute of the Metropolitan Museum of Art in New York City throws a party now known as the Met Gala, an event Reese was invited to. The gala was first held in 1948 as a midnight dinner. It grew into a fashion event attended by stars from different walks of life when *Vogue* magazine started to work with the Met. Today, attendees often try to interpret the theme of the latest Costume Institute exhibits, which has inspired memorable looks from celebrities including Princess Diana, Zendaya, Beyoncé, and Lady Gaga.

Each year, the Met Gala has a theme that guides how attendees dress. The theme of the 2024 Met Gala was "Sleeping Beauties: Reawakening Fashion."

Sky roster, Reese reached out to the one person she knew would always be in her corner: her mother.

"I was like, 'Angel, just take a deep breath,'" Webb Reese recalled to her daughter on her podcast. "I was like, 'Study on the plane while the young lady's doing your makeup. Study, study, study. . . . Because you wanna graduate. I want you to graduate.'"[2]

Reese did as her mother said. On May 6, her twenty-second birthday, Reese took a private jet right after Sky practice in Chicago's north suburbs. A makeup artist and hairstylist flew with her, helping her get ready while on the plane.

Reese worked with Naomi Elizeé, the same stylist who came up with her looks for the *Vogue* shoot and draft night to pick out her dress, a mint-green gown from the brand 16Arlington. She was the first WNBA rookie to walk the red carpet for the Met Gala and just the second WNBA player to attend. "I love using fashion as a vehicle for creativity and expression in everything I do," Reese said. "It's been amazing to have the fashion industry really embrace the WNBA—and female athletes overall."[3]

PLAYING IN THE WNBA

The day after the Met Gala, Reese was back on the court to play in the Sky's preseason game against the New York Liberty. She had 13 points and five rebounds in less than 20 minutes in the game. Preseason games are opportunities for all the players to show what they can do, so Reese played fewer minutes than she usually did in college.

After training camp, the Sky announced their final roster, and Reese indeed had made the team. The regular season began with a game in Dallas on May 15. But Reese would be starting the season without fellow rookie Kamilla Cardoso. A shoulder injury sustained in the first preseason game put Cardoso on the bench for six weeks.

Though starting the WNBA season was a dream come true for Reese, she was missing out on an important milestone. LSU's graduation fell on the first weekend of the WNBA season, so she didn't get to walk across the stage to accept her diploma. Instead, she shared pictures on social media announcing her graduation.

Reese's first month in the WNBA started well, coming with lots of learning opportunities as she figured out how the game was different from what she had played in college. She scored in the double digits in her first five games of the season and notched her first double-double on May 28 in a loss to Seattle. She said, "It's been great.

HISTORY OF THE CHICAGO SKY

In February 2005, the NBA announced that Chicago was awarded a WNBA franchise. Unlike most other WNBA teams at the time, the Chicago franchise would not have the same owner as the Chicago Bulls, the city's NBA team. Instead, the ownership group was led by real estate developer Michael Alter. Named the Sky in honor of Chicago's iconic skyline, the Sky has been the home of WNBA greats such as Sylvia Fowles, Elena Delle Donne, Courtney Vandersloot, and Candace Parker. The team won its first championship in 2021 and drafted Reese in 2024.

Just being able to affect the game in different ways, understanding the transition and just giving myself grace and being patient with everything. I've been able to have fun out there and grow every game."[4]

On June 1, the Sky headed to Indiana for a matchup WNBA fans were excited about. The Sky would play the Fever. The game was not just about two young teams facing off. It was one more chapter in the rivalry between Reese and Caitlin Clark.

Playing at Gainbridge Fieldhouse in Indianapolis, Indiana, Reese and Clark had relatively quiet games as the Fever defeated the Sky 71–70. The game had one controversial moment that ended up fueling a national conversation. Chennedy Carter, Reese's teammate, threw her hip into Clark, who fell to the ground. Carter was immediately given a foul, and the game went on.

Tickets for the Sky–Fever game on June 1 sold out ahead of the matchup.

After the game, people who were not used to the physicality of the WNBA were shocked by the foul. Carter was called a bully. Analysts accused WNBA veterans of not being appreciative enough of Clark.

A week after the foul, Clark tried to bring the focus back to basketball. "Sometimes it stinks how much the conversation is outside of basketball and not the product on the floor and the amazing players that are on the floor and how good they are for their teams and how great this season has been for women's basketball," she said.[5]

> "I think so many people are watching women's basketball right now. It all started from the national championship game, and I've been dealing with this for two years now and understand that, yeah, negative things have probably been said about me. But honestly, I'll take that because look where women's basketball is."[6]
>
> —Angel Reese, June 2024

Back on the court, things were not going so well for the Sky in early June. While the team did have a healthy Cardoso back, it was struggling to close out wins. Reese was ejected in a game against the Liberty after a referee gave her two technical fouls for her reaction to a foul call. WNBA players are fined for technical fouls. The next day, it was reported that Reese's second foul had been rescinded by the league. She would only have to pay a fine for her first foul.

The Sky won one game and lost six in the first half of June. With so many new players on the team, they needed time to gel. In a home game on June 20 against the Dallas Wings, the Sky finally started to come together. Reese scored 16 points, had 18 rebounds, and grabbed two steals. It was her seventh consecutive double-double, breaking a WNBA rookie record.

Reese's coach, Weatherspoon, had expected the rookie to find success. "I'm not surprised at all," Weatherspoon said after Reese's performance against the Wings. "The moment you sit down and get to know this young lady as a person, what her desires are and why she's so hungry to do what she does between those four lines, it makes a difference."[7]

The streak continued. On July 2, Reese's hard work was recognized by

TERESA WEATHERSPOON

After a long career playing basketball overseas, Teresa Weatherspoon returned to the United States in 1997 with the start of the WNBA. Playing for the New York Liberty, she won the first WNBA Defensive Player of the Year award. She started coaching in 2007, and in 2019, she was hired to the coaching staff of the New Orleans Pelicans in the NBA. In 2023, she was hired by the Chicago Sky and coached Reese for one season.

the league's players, media, and fans. She was just one of two rookies named to the All-Star team. The other rookie was Clark. Finally, they would play together as All-Star teammates instead of facing each other.

Reese said, "I'm just so happy. I know the work I put in. Coming into this league, so many people doubted me and didn't think my game would translate and I wouldn't be the player that I was in college or would be worse and wouldn't be where I am right now."[8]

TAKING ON TEAM USA

Because 2024 was an Olympic year, the All-Star game had a different format than usual. The All-Star team faced the US Olympic team as a warm-up before Team USA headed to Paris to try to win Olympic gold. Though Reese wasn't a starter, she still managed a double-double with 12 points and 11 rebounds.

In one memorable moment, Clark dished the ball on a bounce pass around Brittney Griner to Reese for a layup, showing what could happen when the two players team up. After the game, Reese said, "I haven't checked my phone yet, but my phone is blowing up. I know that bucket went [viral]. [Clark] even said on the bench, 'You know how many people are happy right now?'"[9]

Team WNBA won the game 117–109. The game clearly helped Team USA prepare for the Olympics. The team went on to win its eighth consecutive gold medal, breaking a record for team sports at the Olympics.

The Olympic break meant Reese and her teammates could take time to relax. She found ways to have fun during the break, including attending the Lollapalooza music festival in downtown Chicago in August. Reese surprised her friend, rapper Megan Thee Stallion, on the stage during her set.

Reese also solidified her offseason plans during the Olympic break. Two WNBA stars, Breanna Stewart and Napheesa Collier, were starting a new basketball league called Unrivaled. The league would give their colleagues a place to play three-on-three basketball during the WNBA offseason without having to look for opportunities in other countries.

Reese decided to join the new league because of the salary and the ability to stay in the United States. "A lot of us never want to go overseas, but some people do have to unfortunately," she said. "So being able to make six figures here within three months, being able to be housed in Miami, just being able to get better at 3-on-3—that's something that I love to do."[10]

Clark scored only four points in the All-Star game, but she did record ten assists, including one that allowed Reese to score.

After the Olympics, the Sky struggled despite Reese's continued double-doubles. She became the first person in WNBA history to earn 20 or more rebounds in back-to-back games—then she stretched the streak to three games. By the end of the season, she had broken the WNBA rookie record for rebounds and the all-time WNBA record for rebounds per game.

Unfortunately for Reese, the season ended well before she had hoped. In a game against the Los Angeles Sparks, Reese suffered a wrist injury that required season-ending surgery. She fell after making a contested layup, breaking her fall with her hands. She continued to play in the game

Reese's wrist injury required her to wear a cast for six weeks.

after the fall, hitting a three-pointer late in the victory against the Sparks, but she later learned that she had cracked a bone in her wrist. "I never would have imagined the last bucket of my rookie season would be a three. Maybe that was God saying, 'Give them a taste of what they will be seeing more of in Year 2,'" she wrote on social media in announcing the injury.[11]

The Sky ended the season on a five-game losing streak. Weatherspoon was fired after just one year as the head coach of the team. A season that had started with so much promise ended in disappointment. However, Reese had shown she belonged in the WNBA. In fact, she quickly became one of its biggest stars.

CHAPTER EIGHT

OFF THE COURT

With the Chicago Sky season over, Reese had time to put into other projects she cared about. For the first time since before her senior season at LSU, Reese was getting a real break from playing basketball. This opened the door for Reese to focus on work away from the court, including a podcast and sponsorships.

Before she even started at Maryland, Reese spoke of her ambitions of becoming a broadcaster. In September 2024, she released the first episode of *Unapologetically Angel*, a podcast on which she talked with a variety of guests. In the episode, she spoke candidly with producer Maya Reese, an experienced sports content creator who is not related to Angel, about her first season, her thoughts on Caitlin Clark, and how Clark's fans have treated her.

Reese wore a top combining jerseys for the Lynx and the Liberty to show support for both teams during their playoff matchup. >>

MINNES

"Caitlin is an amazing player and I've always thought she was an amazing player," Reese said.

> *I think it's really just the fans, her fans, the Iowa fans, now the Indiana fans, that are, like, they ride for her and I respect that, respectfully, but sometimes it's very disrespectful. I think there's a lot of racism when it comes to it and I don't believe she stands on any of that.*[1]

Reese continued releasing weekly episodes. She spoke with Dwyane Wade, basketball Hall of Famer and partial owner of the Chicago Sky, about the sacrifices they made to be basketball players. Reese talked to the rapper GloRilla about dating. And when Reese had her mother as a guest, she broke the news that she had paid off her mother's mortgage.

ATHLETES WITH PODCASTS

Angel Reese is far from the only athlete with a podcast. Brothers Jason and Travis Kelce, both NFL football players, have a popular podcast that was once valued at more than $100 million.[2] Megan Rapinoe and Sue Bird, athletes who are also a couple, host the podcast *A Touch More*.

Money has been a subject Reese has not shied away from, whether it was telling her mom that she can retire or discussing her WNBA salary. In an Instagram livestream in October 2024, Reese said, "I just hope y'all know, the

Reese appeared on the box of a limited edition of Reese's Puffs cereal in October 2024.

WNBA don't pay my bills at all. I don't even think it pays one of my bills. Literally."[3]

Instead of relying on her WNBA rookie contract, which in its first year made Reese around $75,000, she makes the bulk of her money through endorsements.[4] Some of these endorsements, such as Reebok and Beats by Dre, started when she was still in college. Others are newer.

Reese long called her fans the "Reese's Pieces," after the peanut butter–filled candy. In August 2024, she announced a deal with the candy company to create cobranded merchandise. The beginnings of this deal had

DC Power FC's first season in the USL began on August 17, 2024.

emerged in June, when Reese posted on social media, "Reese's pieces, where y'all at?"[5] Fans started asking Reese's social media accounts about a partnership. She wore a custom pair of basketball shoes with a Reese's Pieces theme for a Sky game against the Minnesota Lynx. Two months later, the partnership was announced.

Reese's Pieces wasn't the only brand Reese engaged with. She also signed an endorsement deal with McDonald's to promote a custom meal, making her the first female athlete to get such a deal. The meal featured McDonald's signature quarter pounder with cheese, plus bacon and barbecue sauce. Along with the burger, the meal featured french fries and Hi-C Orange Lavaburst to drink.

All these endorsements meant Reese could put her money toward an investment she cared about. Still thinking of her Maryland roots, Reese became a founding investor in the DC Power Football Club (FC). This was a new franchise in the upstart women's United Soccer League (USL) Super League.

She said, "I want to help grow women's sports and elevate female athletes across the board. We're taking over, and I'm honored to be able to support Power FC and invest in women's soccer in the DMV [District of Columbia, Maryland, and Virginia] community."[6]

Reese also had a chance in the offseason for another *Vogue* photo shoot. Unlike the one in which she announced she was heading to the WNBA, this shoot was part of a bigger story on how athletes were getting into fashion. She was on the cover in a red dress by Versace. "It's always been both: basketball and fashion,"

THE USL SUPER LEAGUE

Reese's DC Power FC is part of the USL Super League. In 2024, the US Soccer Federation granted the league Division I sanctioning. This puts the USL Super League on the same level as the National Women's Soccer League (NWSL), which had been the only Division I league. DC Power FC plays at Audi Field, which is also home to the Washington Spirit, a team in the NWSL.

Reese said. "But I was a fashion girlie from young too. . . . I was always in my mom's closet, putting on her stuff. I liked to carry a purse. Hair done. I wanted to look put together. I still do."[7]

WHERE CAN WNBA PLAYERS PLAY IN THE OFFSEASON?

Beginning in 2025, the WNBA season includes 44 games, so players often look for offseason opportunities to improve their game and make more money. Until recently, players would head to leagues in Europe, Australia, and China. Reese said she didn't want to go overseas, so she chose from the two offseason leagues in the United States, Unrivaled and Athletes Unlimited. These options give players more flexibility in offseason play.

UNRIVALED

In January 2025, it was time for Reese to return to basketball. She had signed on with the new Unrivaled basketball league. Support from investors including Olympic swimming legend Michael Phelps, women's soccer star Alex Morgan, and tennis superstar Coco Gauff allowed the league to offer six-figure salaries and state-of-the-art facilities for its 36 players.

Reese was drafted by the Rose Basketball Club. Unrivaled features a different style of basketball than the WNBA, with three-on-three play on a smaller court. It didn't take Reese long to adjust her play. In her first game, she had 10 points and 14 rebounds.

Playing on a team with Chelsea Gray, Kahleah Copper, and Azurá Stevens, all WNBA champions, Reese began to truly excel on the court. Basketball Hall of Famer Lisa Leslie worked as one of Unrivaled's commentators. She appeared on Reese's podcast with some tough but helpful advice.

"The biggest advice I have for you is gonna be how you shoot your layups, period. We're gonna fix that," Leslie said.[8] True to her word, Reese and Leslie spent time on the court, with Leslie helping Reese in the paint.

Reese continued to make waves with Unrivaled during its eight-week season. On February 21, 2025, she became the first Unrivaled player to score 20 points and have 20 rebounds

Reese wore the number five on her Rose jersey in the Unrivaled league.

Playing against the Connecticut Sun on June 15, 2025, Reese recorded her first WNBA triple-double.

in one game. "Being able to see my growth, I put in the work, and a lot of people don't see what I put in," she said. "It's great to see the results out there. But obviously, I'm not done yet."[9]

She wasn't close to done yet. Reese continued to earn double-doubles. At the end of the regular season, she was named the Unrivaled Defensive Player of the Year (DPOY). Even while playing in the same league as previous WNBA DPOYs Brittney Griner and Collier, Reese's defensive play stood out.

Still in her early twenties, Reese had already become a superstar on and off the court, and she was just getting started. At her young age, she had shown amazing potential. Fans wondered whether a WNBA championship or an Olympic gold medal was in her future. Reese had shown anything is possible.

ESSENTIAL FACTS

Full Name: Angel Reese

Date of Birth: May 6, 2002

Place of Birth: Randallstown, Maryland

Parents: Michael Reese and Angel Webb Reese

Education: Saint Frances Academy, University of Maryland, Louisiana State University

RISE TO STARDOM

- As a child, Reese joined Team Takeover, an Amateur Athletic Union (AAU) basketball program. In high school, she was a standout player for Saint Frances Academy.
- The University of Maryland Terrapins recruited Reese. She played with the Terrapins for two seasons.
- In 2022, Reese transferred to Louisiana State University (LSU) to play with the Tigers.

CAREER HIGHLIGHTS

- In 2023, Reese led LSU to the Tigers' first NCAA title and was named the tournament's Most Outstanding Player.
- Reese was selected by the Chicago Sky in the 2024 WNBA Draft. In her first season in the WNBA, she broke the WNBA's single-season rebounding record and was named an All-Star.

- After her first WNBA season, she became an Unrivaled champion and was named the Unrivaled Defensive Player of the Year. Reese also signed sponsorship deals with Reese's and McDonald's.

TEAMS

- Saint Frances Academy Panthers (2017–2020)
- University of Maryland Terrapins (2020–2022)
- Louisiana State University Tigers (2022–2024)
- Chicago Sky (2024–)
- Rose Basketball Club (2025–)

QUOTE

"I've done everything I wanted to in college. I've won a national championship, I've gotten SEC Player of the Year, I've been an All-American. My ultimate goal is to be a pro—and to be one of the greatest basketball players to play, ever. I feel like I'm ready."

—Angel Reese, April 2024, declaring that she would enter the WNBA Draft

GLOSSARY

cagey
Hesitant to reveal information.

collective bargaining
The process by which an employer and a labor union negotiate details of employment such as wages.

commissioner
The head of a professional sports league.

consecutive
Occurring in a row.

draft
An event in which professional sports teams gain exclusive rights to new players.

endorsement
A form of advertising in which a person, usually a celebrity, publicly declares support for a product or service.

extravagant
Going beyond what is reasonable or necessary.

inducted
Admitted into a position or organization.

lucrative
Profitable.

phenomenon
A notable person or event.

prevail
To succeed against.

prospect
A candidate for a position.

raucous
Disorderly.

recreational
Relating to an activity done for enjoyment outside work.

rescind
To take back.

rivalry
A long-term competitive relationship between two or more athletes or teams.

scrimmage
An informal sports game played for practice.

upstart
Someone or something that has gained sudden notability.

ADDITIONAL RESOURCES

SELECTED BIBLIOGRAPHY

Cooper, Leah Faye. "Angel Reese Is Taking Her Talents to the WNBA." *Vogue*, 1 Apr. 2023, vogue.com. Accessed 21 May 2025.

Peter, Josh. "There's More to LSU Star Angel Reese Than Trash-Talking Women's Basketball National Champion." *USA Today*, 13 Apr. 2023, usatoday.com. Accessed 21 May 2025.

Philippou, Alexa. "Angel Reese Embracing Patience, Growth in Rookie WNBA Season." *ESPN*, 31 May 2024, espn.com. Accessed 21 May 2025.

FURTHER READINGS

Clendenan, Megan. *Caitlin Clark*. Abdo, 2026.

Hoehn, Jim. *WNBA*. Abdo, 2021.

Johnson, Mike. *Inspirational Basketball Stories for Young Readers: 12 Unbelievable True Tales to Inspire and Amaze Young Basketball Lovers*. Curious Press, 2023.

ONLINE RESOURCES

To learn more about Angel Reese, please visit **abdobooklinks.com** or scan this QR code. These links are routinely monitored and updated to provide the most current information available.

MORE INFORMATION

For more information on this subject, contact or visit the following organizations:

ANGEL C. REESE FOUNDATION

3608 Offutt Rd., PO Box 574
Randallstown, MD 21133
angelcreesefoundation.org

The Angel C. Reese Foundation's mission is to promote equality for girls in sports, education, and other areas.

CHICAGO SKY

200 E. Cermak Rd.
Chicago, IL 60616
sky.wnba.com

Fans can visit the website of the Chicago Sky to purchase tickets and merchandise. They can also learn about the team and its players.

WOMEN'S BASKETBALL HALL OF FAME

700 S. Hall of Fame Dr.
Knoxville, TN 37915
wbhof.com

Located in Knoxville, Tennessee, the Women's Basketball Hall of Fame is a museum showcasing women's greatest accomplishments on the court.

SOURCE NOTES

CHAPTER 1. THE FINAL FOUR

1. Law Roach. "'We Love a Tall Girl:' Angel Reese Meets Law Roach." *Interview*, 1 Nov. 2023, interviewmagazine.com. Accessed 26 June 2025.
2. "LSU Final Four Postgame Press Conference—2023 NCAA Tournament." *YouTube*, uploaded by March Madness, 31 Mar. 2023, youtube.com. Accessed 26 June 2025.
3. "Mulkey, LSU Women Rally in Final Four, Reach 1st Title Game." *ESPN*, 31 Mar. 2023, espn.com. Accessed 26 June 2025.
4. "LSU Final Four Postgame Press Conference."

CHAPTER 2. EARLY YEARS

1. "2024–25 UMBC Women's Basketball Record Book." *University of Maryland, Baltimore County*, 5 Feb. 2025, umbcretrievers.com. Accessed 26 June 2025.
2. "Angel Retires Her Mom & Pays Off Her Mortgage." *Unapologetically Angel*, 30 Jan. 2025, youtube.com.
3. "Angel Retires Her Mom."
4. "Angel Retires Her Mom."
5. Tom Worgo. "An Interview with Angel Reese." *What's Up? Media*, 8 Mar. 2022, whatsupmag.com. Accessed 26 June 2025.
6. "Angel Retires Her Mom."
7. "Angel Retires Her Mom."
8. "Angel Retires Her Mom."

CHAPTER 3. HIGH SCHOOL AND RECRUITING

1. Jeremy Goldstein. "Angel Reese Shows True Colors as Inspiring High School Speech Emerges." *Mirror US*, 25 Sept. 2024, themirror.com. Accessed 26 June 2025.
2. Glenn Graham. "2019–20 High School Female Athlete of the Year." *Baltimore Sun*, 25 May 2020, baltimoresun.com. Accessed 26 June 2025.
3. Walter Villa. "No. 2 Senior Prospect Angel Reese Narrows College List to Five." *ESPN*, 19 June 2019, espn.com. Accessed 26 June 2025.
4. "Terrapins Sign Angel Reese, No. 2 Overall Recruit." *University of Maryland Athletics*, 13 Nov. 2019, umterps.com. Accessed 26 June 2025.
5. Cassandra Negley. "No. 2 Recruit Angel Reese Target of Discrediting Remarks." *Yahoo Sports*, 17 Jan. 2020, sports.yahoo.com. Accessed 26 June 2025.
6. Jerry Bembry. "Top Prospect Angel Reese the Target of Offensive Messages." *Andscape*, 17 Jan. 2020, andscape.com. Accessed 26 June 2025.

CHAPTER 4. MARYLAND TERRAPIN

1. Edward Lee. "Maryland Women's Basketball Leaning on New Players to Drive Program, Led by St. Frances Star Angel Reese." *Baltimore Sun*, 11 Nov. 2020, baltimoresun.com. Accessed 26 June 2025.

2. Katherine Fominykh. "Maryland Women's Basketball Overwhelms Iowa, 111–93." *Baltimore Sun*, 23 Feb. 2021, baltimoresun.com. Accessed 26 June 2025.

3. Chantel Jennings. "Maryland's Angel Reese Is Back from Injury." *New York Times*, 18 Nov. 2021, nytimes.com. Accessed 26 June 2025.

4. @Reese10Angel. "I took the scariest step of my life!" *X*, 5 Apr. 2023, 8:48 p.m., x.com. Accessed 26 June 2025.

CHAPTER 5. LOUISIANA STATE TIGER

1. Harrison Valentine. "Kim Mulkey Is Home." *Louisiana State University*, 26 Apr. 2021, lsusports.net. Accessed 26 June 2025.

2. Alexa Philippou. "LSU Lands Women's Basketball Transfer Angel Reese." *ESPN*, 6 May 2022, espn.com. Accessed 26 June 2025.

3. Philippou, "LSU Lands Women's Basketball Transfer Angel Reese."

4. Jim Kleinpeter. "Kim Mulkey: We Have Talent and Now Must 'Piece It Together.'" *NOLA*, 26 Sept. 2022, nola.com. Accessed 26 June 2025.

5. "Reese Eclipses 1,000 Career Points as LSU Rolls through OSU, 87–55." *Louisiana State University*, 19 Dec. 2022, lsusports.net. Accessed 26 June 2025.

6. Jim Kleinpeter. "Angel Reese Having Breakout Season." *NOLA*, 27 Dec. 2022, nola.com. Accessed 26 June 2025.

7. Scott Rabalais. "Time to Turn the Page and Find Out How Good Kim Mulkey's LSU Team Is." *NOLA*, 28 Dec. 2022, nola.com. Accessed 26 June 2025.

8. Evan Easterling. "LSU Buoyed by Trash-Talking, Shot-Swishing Angel Reese." *New York Times*, 2 Mar. 2023, nytimes.com. Accessed 26 June 2025.

9. Remy Tumin and Alanis Thames. "Pretty in Any Color." *New York Times*, 24 July 2022, nytimes.com. Accessed 26 June 2025.

10. Natasha Dye. "LSU Star Angel Reese Responds to Critics." *People*, 3 Apr. 2023, people.com. Accessed 26 June 2025.

11. Ben Morse. "Caitlin Clark Defends Angel Reese." *CNN*, 5 Apr. 2023, cnn.com. Accessed 26 June 2025.

12. Candace Parker. "Angel Reese." *Time*, 13 Sept. 2023, time.com. Accessed 26 June 2025.

13. Ricky O'Donnell. "Angel Reese's Absence and Return for LSU, Explained by What We Know." *SB Nation*, 30 Nov. 2023, sbnation.com. Accessed 26 June 2025.

SOURCE NOTES

14. @Reese10Angel. "please don't believe everything you read." *X*, 19 Nov. 2023, 11:23 a.m., x.com. Accessed 26 June 2025.

15. Patrick Magee. "LSU's Angel Reese Explains How Shaquille O'Neal Helped Her." *NOLA*, 1 Dec. 2023, nola.com. Accessed 26 June 2025.

16. Patrick Magee. "LSU's Angel Reese Lets Tears Flow as She Details a Difficult Year." *NOLA*, 1 Apr. 2024, nola.com. Accessed 26 June 2025.

CHAPTER 6. THE 2024 WNBA DRAFT

1. Brett Martel. "LSU Star Angel Reese Declares for WNBA Draft via Vogue Photo Shoot, Says 'I Didn't Want to Be Basic.'" *Associated Press*, 3 Apr. 2024, apnews.com. Accessed 26 June 2025.

2. Martel, "Angel Reese Declares for WNBA Draft."

3. @Reese10Angel. "the best part of the weekend in NYC was getting to know all the girls after being sooo competitive for the last 4 years!!" *X*, 17 Apr. 2024, 9:58 p.m., x.com. Accessed 26 June 2025.

4. Christen A. Johnson. "Exclusive: 10 Minutes with Angel Reese." *Cosmopolitan*, 16 Apr. 2024, cosmopolitan.com. Accessed 26 June 2025.

5. Johnson, "10 Minutes with Angel Reese."

6. Leah Faye Cooper. "Angel Reese Is Taking Her Talents to the WNBA." *Vogue*, 3 Apr. 2024, vogue.com. Accessed 26 June 2025.

7. "Bayou Barbie Angel Reese Selected No. 7 Overall." *YouTube*, uploaded by ESPN, 15 Apr. 2024, youtube.com. Accessed 26 June 2025.

8. "Chicago Sky Select Angel Reese with No. 7 Overall Pick." *Chicago Sky*, 16 Apr. 2024, sky.wnba.com. Accessed 26 June 2025.

9. Rick Tarsitano. "Sky Rookie Angel Reese Sparks Ticket & Jersey Sales to Skyrocket." *WGN9*, 24 Apr. 2024, wgntv.com. Accessed 26 June 2025.

CHAPTER 7. CHICAGO SKY

1. Julia Poe. "Angel Reese Isn't Taking Anything for Granted." *Chicago Tribune*, 24 Apr. 2024, chicagotribune.com. Accessed 26 June 2025.

2. "Angel Retires Her Mom & Pays Off Her Mortgage." *Unapologetically Angel*, 30 Jan. 2025, youtube.com.

3. Leah Faye Cooper. "Angel Reese Got Ready for the 2024 Met Gala on a Private Jet." *Vogue*, 7 May 2024, vogue.com. Accessed 26 June 2025.

4. Alexa Philippou. "Angel Reese Embracing Patience, Growth." *ESPN*, 31 May 2024, espn.com. Accessed 26 June 2025.

5. Christine Brennan. "Caitlin Clark Reacts to Controversy." *USA Today*, 8 June 2024, usatoday.com. Accessed 26 June 2025.

CONTINUED. . .

6. Ingrid Vasquez. "Angel Reese Talks Caitlin Clark." *Yahoo Sports*, 3 June 2024, sports.yahoo.com. Accessed 26 June 2025.

7. Annie Costabile. "Angel Reese Makes WNBA History as First Rookie with Seven Consecutive Double-Doubles." *Chicago Sun-Times*, 20 June 2024, chicago.suntimes.com. Accessed 26 June 2025.

8. Julia Poe. "Chicago Sky's Angel Reese Is Named to the WNBA All-Star Team." *Chicago Tribune*, 3 July 2024, chicagotribune.com. Accessed 26 June 2025.

9. Annie Costabile. "Angel Reese Gets Another Double-Double in Team WNBA's All-Star Win over Team USA." *Chicago Sun-Times*, 20 June 2024, chicago.suntimes.com. Accessed 26 June 2025.

10. Julia Poe. "Former Sky Players Star in Gold Medal Game—and Angel Reese Sets 'Unrivaled' Offseason Plans." *Chicago Tribune*, 12 Aug. 2024, chicagotribune.com. Accessed 26 June 2025.

11. Annie Costabile. "Sky Rookie Angel Reese to Miss Rest of Season with Wrist Injury." *Chicago Sun-Times*, 7 Sept. 2024, chicago.suntimes.com. Accessed 26 June 2025.

CHAPTER 8. OFF THE COURT

1. Zachary Draves. "Angel Reese Is Following the Tradition of Black Athletes and Reclaiming Her Story." *Swish Appeal*, 6 Sept. 2024, swishappeal.com. Accessed 26 June 2025.

2. "Jason Kelce, Travis Kelce Reportedly Sign $100M+ Podcast Deal." *ESPN*, 27 Aug. 2024, espn.com. Accessed 26 June 2025.

3. Michele Steele. "Sky Forward Angel Reese: 'The WNBA Don't Pay My Bills.'" *ESPN*, 17 Oct. 2024, espn.com. Accessed 26 June 2025.

4. "WNBA Rookie Scale." *Spotrac*, n.d., spotrac.com. Accessed 26 June 2025.

5. Liz Roscher. "Sky's Angel Reese Partners with Reese's Pieces to Create Perfect Logo Mashup Collection." *Yahoo Sports*, 21 Aug. 2024, sports.yahoo.com. Accessed 26 June 2025.

6. Liz Roscher. "Angel Reese, Aspiring Business Mogul, Named Newest Part-Owner of DC Power FC." *Yahoo Sports*, 21 May 2024, sports.yahoo.com. Accessed 26 June 2025.

7. Maya Singer. "How Sports and Fashion Fell in Love." *Vogue*, 8 Jan. 2025, vogue.com. Accessed 26 June 2025.

8. "Lisa Leslie." *Basketball Hall of Fame*, n.d. hoophall.com. Accessed 26 June 2025.

9. "Sky's Angel Reese Makes Unrivaled History with First 20–20 Game in Win." *Chicago Sun-Times*, 21 Feb. 2024, chicago.suntimes.com. Accessed 26 June 2025.

INDEX

ABOUT THE AUTHOR

MAGGIE HENDRICKS

Maggie Hendricks is a versatile and passionate reporter on all sports—and especially women's athletics. Over her nearly two-decade career, she also has hosted a weekly radio show on 670 The Score in Chicago and worked for the Olympics, Bally Sports, Yahoo Sports, the Athletic, and *USA Today*. Her work has been noted by the Best American Sports Writing, Associated Press Sports Editors, and the Gracie Awards.